Dog Informations

Name:

Breed:

Color(s):

Eye color:

Special Marketing:

Microchip:

Dog Tag Registration:

Weight:

Height:

Blood Type:

Medications:

Allergies & Illness:

Other details:

# Veterenarian Infos

Name:	
Address:	
Phone:	
Email:	

Vaccinations	Date

Vet Visits

Date: _____ Age: _____

Reason for Visit: _____

_____

_____

Tests Done:

_____

_____

_____

Diagnosis:

_____

_____

_____

Medication - Vaccinations:

_____

_____

_____

Comments:

_____

_____

_____

Vet Visits

Date: _____ Age: _____

Reason for Visit: _____

_____

_____

Tests Done:

_____

_____

_____

Diagnosis:

_____

_____

_____

Medication - Vaccinations:

_____

_____

_____

Comments:

_____

_____

_____

Vet Visits

Date: _____ Age: _____

Reason for Visit: _____

_____

Tests Done: _____

_____

_____

Diagnosis: _____

_____

_____

Medication - Vaccinations: _____

_____

_____

Comments: _____

_____

_____

Vet Visits

Date: _____ Age: _____

Reason for Visit: _____

_____

_____

Tests Done:

_____

_____

_____

Diagnosis:

_____

_____

_____

Medication - Vaccinations:

_____

_____

_____

Comments:

_____

_____

_____

Vet Visits

Date: _____ Age: _____

Reason for Visit: _____

_____

_____

Tests Done:

_____

_____

_____

Diagnosis:

_____

_____

_____

Medication - Vaccinations:

_____

_____

_____

Comments:

_____

_____

_____

Vet Visits

Date: _____ Age: _____

Reason for Visit: _____

_____

_____

Tests Done:

_____

_____

_____

Diagnosis:

_____

_____

_____

Medication - Vaccinations:

_____

_____

_____

Comments:

_____

_____

_____

Vet Visits

Date: _____ Age: _____

Reason for Visit: _____

_____

_____

Tests Done:

_____

_____

_____

Diagnosis:

_____

_____

_____

Medication - Vaccinations:

_____

_____

_____

Comments:

_____

_____

_____

Vet Visits

Date: _____ Age: _____

Reason for Visit: _____

_____

_____

Tests Done:

_____

_____

_____

Diagnosis:

_____

_____

_____

Medication - Vaccinations:

_____

_____

_____

Comments:

_____

_____

_____

Vet Visits

Date: _____ **Age:** _____

Reason for Visit: _____

_____

_____

Tests Done:

_____

_____

_____

Diagnosis:

_____

_____

_____

Medication - Vaccinations:

_____

_____

_____

Comments:

_____

_____

_____

Vet Visits

Date:	Age:

Reason for Visit:

Tests Done:

Diagnosis:

Medication - Vaccinations:

Comments:

Vet Visits

Date: _____ Age: _____

Reason for Visit: _____
_____
_____

Tests Done:
_____
_____
_____

Diagnosis:
_____
_____
_____

Medication - Vaccinations:
_____
_____
_____

Comments:
_____
_____
_____

Vet Visits

Date:	Age:
Reason for Visit:	

Tests Done:

_____

_____

_____

Diagnosis:

_____

_____

_____

Medication - Vaccinations:

_____

_____

_____

Comments:

_____

_____

_____

Vet Visits

Date: _____ Age: _____

Reason for Visit: _____

_____

_____

Tests Done:

_____

_____

_____

Diagnosis:

_____

_____

_____

Medication - Vaccinations:

_____

_____

_____

Comments:

_____

_____

_____

Vet Visits

Date: _____ Age: _____

Reason for Visit: _____

_____

_____

Tests Done:

_____

_____

_____

Diagnosis:

_____

_____

_____

Medication - Vaccinations:

_____

_____

_____

Comments:

_____

_____

_____

Vet Visits

Date: _____ Age: _____

Reason for Visit: _____

_____

_____

Tests Done:

_____

_____

_____

Diagnosis:

_____

_____

_____

Medication - Vaccinations:

_____

_____

_____

Comments:

_____

_____

_____

Vet Visits

Date: _____ Age: _____

Reason for Visit: _____

_____

_____

Tests Done:

_____

_____

_____

Diagnosis:

_____

_____

_____

Medication - Vaccinations:

_____

_____

_____

Comments:

_____

_____

_____

Vet Visits

Date: _____ Age: _____

Reason for Visit: _____
_____
_____

Tests Done:
_____
_____
_____

Diagnosis:
_____
_____
_____

Medication - Vaccinations:
_____
_____
_____

Comments:
_____
_____
_____

Vet Visits

Date: _____ Age: _____

Reason for Visit: _____

_____

_____

Tests Done:

_____

_____

_____

Diagnosis:

_____

_____

_____

Medication - Vaccinations:

_____

_____

_____

Comments:

_____

_____

_____

Vet Visits

Date: _____ Age: _____

Reason for Visit: _____
_____
_____

Tests Done:
_____
_____
_____

Diagnosis:
_____
_____
_____

Medication - Vaccinations:
_____
_____
_____

Comments:
_____
_____
_____

Vet Visits

Date: _____ Age: _____

Reason for Visit: _____

_____

_____

Tests Done:

_____

_____

_____

Diagnosis:

_____

_____

_____

Medication - Vaccinations:

_____

_____

_____

Comments:

_____

_____

_____

Vet Visits

Date: _____ Age: _____

Reason for Visit: _____
_____
_____

Tests Done:
_____
_____
_____

Diagnosis:
_____
_____
_____

Medication - Vaccinations:
_____
_____
_____

Comments:
_____
_____
_____

Vet Visits

Date:	Age:

Reason for Visit:

Tests Done:

Diagnosis:

Medication - Vaccinations:

Comments:

Vet Visits

Date: _____ Age: _____

Reason for Visit: _____

_____

_____

Tests Done:

_____

_____

_____

Diagnosis:

_____

_____

_____

Medication - Vaccinations:

_____

_____

_____

Comments:

_____

_____

_____

Vet Visits

Date: _____ Age: _____

Reason for Visit: _____
_____
_____

Tests Done:
_____
_____
_____

Diagnosis:
_____
_____
_____

Medication - Vaccinations:
_____
_____
_____

Comments:
_____
_____
_____

Vet Visits

Date: _____ Age: _____

Reason for Visit: _____

_____

_____

Tests Done:

_____

_____

_____

Diagnosis:

_____

_____

_____

Medication - Vaccinations:

_____

_____

_____

Comments:

_____

_____

_____

Vet Visits

Date: _____ Age: _____

Reason for Visit:
_____
_____

Tests Done:
_____
_____
_____

Diagnosis:
_____
_____
_____

Medication - Vaccinations:
_____
_____
_____

Comments:
_____
_____
_____

Vet Visits

Date: _____ Age: _____

Reason for Visit: _____

_____

_____

Tests Done:

_____

_____

_____

Diagnosis:

_____

_____

_____

Medication - Vaccinations:

_____

_____

_____

Comments:

_____

_____

_____

Vet Visits

Date: _____ Age: _____

Reason for Visit: _____

_____

_____

Tests Done:

_____

_____

_____

Diagnosis:

_____

_____

_____

Medication - Vaccinations:

_____

_____

_____

Comments:

_____

_____

_____

Vet Visits

Date: _____ Age: _____

Reason for Visit: _____

_____

_____

Tests Done:

_____

_____

_____

Diagnosis:

_____

_____

_____

Medication - Vaccinations:

_____

_____

_____

Comments:

_____

_____

_____

Vet Visits

Date: _____ Age: _____

Reason for Visit: _____

_____

_____

Tests Done:

_____

_____

_____

Diagnosis:

_____

_____

_____

Medication - Vaccinations:

_____

_____

_____

Comments:

_____

_____

_____

Vet Visits

Date: _____ Age: _____

Reason for Visit: _____

_____

Tests Done:

_____

_____

_____

Diagnosis:

_____

_____

_____

Medication - Vaccinations:

_____

_____

_____

Comments:

_____

_____

_____

Vet Visits

Date: _____ Age: _____

Reason for Visit: _____

_____

Tests Done:

_____

_____

_____

Diagnosis:

_____

_____

_____

Medication - Vaccinations:

_____

_____

_____

Comments:

_____

_____

_____

Vet Visits

Date: _____ Age: _____

Reason for Visit: _____

_____

_____

Tests Done:

_____

_____

_____

Diagnosis:

_____

_____

_____

Medication - Vaccinations:

_____

_____

_____

Comments:

_____

_____

_____

Vet Visits

Date: _____ Age: _____

Reason for Visit: _____

_____

_____

Tests Done:

_____

_____

_____

Diagnosis:

_____

_____

_____

Medication - Vaccinations:

_____

_____

_____

Comments:

_____

_____

_____

Vet Visits

Date: _____ Age: _____

Reason for Visit: _____
_____
_____

Tests Done:
_____
_____
_____

Diagnosis:
_____
_____
_____

Medication - Vaccinations:
_____
_____
_____

Comments:
_____
_____
_____

Vet Visits

Date: _____ Age: _____

Reason for Visit: _____

_____

_____

Tests Done:

_____

_____

_____

Diagnosis:

_____

_____

_____

Medication - Vaccinations:

_____

_____

_____

Comments:

_____

_____

_____

Vet Visits

Date: _____ Age: _____

Reason for Visit: _____

_____

Tests Done:

_____

_____

_____

Diagnosis:

_____

_____

_____

Medication - Vaccinations:

_____

_____

_____

Comments:

_____

_____

_____

Vet Visits

Date: _____ Age: _____

Reason for Visit: _____

_____

_____

Tests Done:

_____

_____

_____

Diagnosis:

_____

_____

_____

Medication - Vaccinations:

_____

_____

_____

Comments:

_____

_____

_____

Vet Visits

Date: _____ Age: _____

Reason for Visit: _____
_____
_____

Tests Done:
_____
_____
_____

Diagnosis:
_____
_____
_____

Medication - Vaccinations:
_____
_____
_____

Comments:
_____
_____
_____

Vet Visits

Date: _____ Age: _____

Reason for Visit: _____

_____

_____

Tests Done:

_____

_____

_____

Diagnosis:

_____

_____

_____

Medication - Vaccinations:

_____

_____

_____

Comments:

_____

_____

_____

Vet Visits

Date: _____   Age: _____

Reason for Visit: _____
_____
_____

Tests Done:
_____
_____
_____

Diagnosis:
_____
_____
_____

Medication - Vaccinations:
_____
_____
_____

Comments:
_____
_____
_____

Vet Visits

Date: _____ Age: _____

Reason for Visit: _____

_____

_____

Tests Done:

_____

_____

_____

Diagnosis:

_____

_____

_____

Medication - Vaccinations:

_____

_____

_____

Comments:

_____

_____

_____

Vet Visits

Date: _____ Age: _____

Reason for Visit: _____

_____

_____

Tests Done:

_____

_____

_____

Diagnosis:

_____

_____

_____

Medication - Vaccinations:

_____

_____

_____

Comments:

_____

_____

_____

Vet Visits

Date: _____ Age: _____

Reason for Visit: _____

_____

_____

Tests Done:

_____

_____

_____

Diagnosis:

_____

_____

_____

Medication - Vaccinations:

_____

_____

_____

Comments:

_____

_____

_____

Vet Visits

Date: _____ Age: _____

Reason for Visit: _____

_____

_____

Tests Done:

_____

_____

_____

Diagnosis:

_____

_____

_____

Medication - Vaccinations:

_____

_____

_____

Comments:

_____

_____

_____

Vet Visits

Date: _____ Age: _____

Reason for Visit: _____

_____

_____

Tests Done:

_____

_____

_____

Diagnosis:

_____

_____

_____

Medication - Vaccinations:

_____

_____

_____

Comments:

_____

_____

_____

Vet Visits

Date: _____ Age: _____

Reason for Visit: _____

_____

_____

Tests Done:

_____

_____

_____

Diagnosis:

_____

_____

_____

Medication - Vaccinations:

_____

_____

_____

Comments:

_____

_____

_____

Vet Visits

Date: _____ Age: _____

Reason for Visit: _____

_____

Tests Done:

_____

_____

_____

Diagnosis:

_____

_____

_____

Medication - Vaccinations:

_____

_____

_____

Comments:

_____

_____

_____

Vet Visits

Date: _____ Age: _____

Reason for Visit: _____
_____
_____

Tests Done:
_____
_____
_____

Diagnosis:
_____
_____
_____

Medication - Vaccinations:
_____
_____
_____

Comments:
_____
_____
_____

Vet Visits

Date: _____ Age: _____

Reason for Visit: _____
_____
_____

Tests Done:
_____
_____
_____

Diagnosis:
_____
_____
_____

Medication - Vaccinations:
_____
_____
_____

Comments:
_____
_____
_____

Vet Visits

Date: _____ Age: _____

Reason for Visit: _____
_____
_____

Tests Done:
_____
_____
_____

Diagnosis:
_____
_____
_____

Medication - Vaccinations:
_____
_____
_____

Comments:
_____
_____
_____

Vet Visits

Date: _____ Age: _____

Reason for Visit: _____

_____

_____

Tests Done:

_____

_____

_____

Diagnosis:

_____

_____

_____

Medication - Vaccinations:

_____

_____

_____

Comments:

_____

_____

_____

Vet Visits

Date: _____ Age: _____

Reason for Visit: _____
_____
_____

Tests Done:
_____
_____
_____

Diagnosis:
_____
_____
_____

Medication - Vaccinations:
_____
_____
_____

Comments:
_____
_____
_____

Vet Visits

Date: _____ Age: _____

Reason for Visit: _____

_____

_____

Tests Done:

_____

_____

_____

Diagnosis:

_____

_____

_____

Medication - Vaccinations:

_____

_____

_____

Comments:

_____

_____

_____

Vet Visits

Date: _____ Age: _____

Reason for Visit: _____
_____
_____

Tests Done:
_____
_____
_____

Diagnosis:
_____
_____
_____

Medication - Vaccinations:
_____
_____
_____

Comments:
_____
_____
_____

Vet Visits

Date: _____ Age: _____

Reason for Visit: _____

_____

_____

Tests Done:

_____

_____

_____

Diagnosis:

_____

_____

_____

Medication - Vaccinations:

_____

_____

_____

Comments:

_____

_____

_____

Vet Visits

Date: _____ Age: _____

Reason for Visit: _____

_____

_____

Tests Done:

_____

_____

_____

Diagnosis:

_____

_____

_____

Medication - Vaccinations:

_____

_____

_____

Comments:

_____

_____

_____

Vet Visits

Date: _____ Age: _____

Reason for Visit: _____

_____

Tests Done:

_____

_____

_____

Diagnosis:

_____

_____

_____

Medication - Vaccinations:

_____

_____

_____

Comments:

_____

_____

_____

Vet Visits

Date: _____ Age: _____

Reason for Visit: _____
_____
_____

Tests Done:
_____
_____
_____

Diagnosis:
_____
_____
_____

Medication - Vaccinations:
_____
_____
_____

Comments:
_____
_____
_____

Vet Visits

Date:	Age:
Reason for Visit:	

Tests Done:

_____

_____

_____

Diagnosis:

_____

_____

_____

Medication - Vaccinations:

_____

_____

_____

Comments:

_____

_____

_____

Vet Visits

Date: _____ Age: _____

Reason for Visit: _____

_____

_____

Tests Done:

_____

_____

_____

Diagnosis:

_____

_____

_____

Medication - Vaccinations:

_____

_____

_____

Comments:

_____

_____

_____

Vet Visits

Date: _____ Age: _____

Reason for Visit: _____
_____
_____

Tests Done:
_____
_____
_____

Diagnosis:
_____
_____
_____

Medication - Vaccinations:
_____
_____
_____

Comments:
_____
_____
_____

Vet Visits

Date: _____ Age: _____

Reason for Visit: _____
_____
_____

Tests Done:
_____
_____
_____

Diagnosis:
_____
_____
_____

Medication - Vaccinations:
_____
_____
_____

Comments:
_____
_____
_____

Vet Visits

Date: _____ Age: _____

Reason for Visit: _____
_____
_____

Tests Done:
_____
_____
_____

Diagnosis:
_____
_____
_____

Medication - Vaccinations:
_____
_____
_____

Comments:
_____
_____
_____

Vet Visits

Date: _____ Age: _____

Reason for Visit: _____

_____

_____

Tests Done:

_____

_____

_____

Diagnosis:

_____

_____

_____

Medication - Vaccinations:

_____

_____

_____

Comments:

_____

_____

_____

Vet Visits

Date: _____ Age: _____

Reason for Visit: _____

_____

_____

Tests Done:

_____

_____

_____

Diagnosis:

_____

_____

_____

Medication - Vaccinations:

_____

_____

_____

Comments:

_____

_____

_____

Vet Visits

Date: _____ Age: _____

Reason for Visit: _____

_____

Tests Done:

_____

_____

_____

Diagnosis:

_____

_____

_____

Medication - Vaccinations:

_____

_____

_____

Comments:

_____

_____

_____

Vet Visits

Date: _____ Age: _____

Reason for Visit: _____

_____

_____

Tests Done:

_____

_____

_____

Diagnosis:

_____

_____

_____

Medication - Vaccinations:

_____

_____

_____

Comments:

_____

_____

_____

Vet Visits

Date: _____ Age: _____

Reason for Visit: _____

_____

_____

Tests Done:

_____

_____

_____

Diagnosis:

_____

_____

_____

Medication - Vaccinations:

_____

_____

_____

Comments:

_____

_____

_____

Vet Visits

Date: _____ Age: _____

Reason for Visit: _____

_____

_____

Tests Done:

_____

_____

_____

Diagnosis:

_____

_____

_____

Medication - Vaccinations:

_____

_____

_____

Comments:

_____

_____

_____

Vet Visits

Date: _____ Age: _____

Reason for Visit: _____

_____

_____

Tests Done:

_____

_____

_____

Diagnosis:

_____

_____

_____

Medication - Vaccinations:

_____

_____

_____

Comments:

_____

_____

_____

Vet Visits

Date: _____ Age: _____

Reason for Visit: _____

_____

_____

Tests Done:

_____

_____

_____

Diagnosis:

_____

_____

_____

Medication - Vaccinations:

_____

_____

_____

Comments:

_____

_____

_____

Vet Visits

Date: _____ Age: _____

Reason for Visit: _____
_____
_____

Tests Done:

_____
_____
_____

Diagnosis:

_____
_____
_____

Medication - Vaccinations:

_____
_____
_____

Comments:

_____
_____
_____

Vet Visits

Date: _____ Age: _____

Reason for Visit: _____

_____

_____

Tests Done:

_____

_____

_____

Diagnosis:

_____

_____

_____

Medication - Vaccinations:

_____

_____

_____

Comments:

_____

_____

_____

Vet Visits

Date: _____ Age: _____

Reason for Visit: _____

_____

_____

Tests Done:

_____

_____

_____

Diagnosis:

_____

_____

_____

Medication - Vaccinations:

_____

_____

_____

Comments:

_____

_____

_____

Vet Visits

Date: _____ Age: _____

Reason for Visit: _____
_____
_____

Tests Done:
_____
_____
_____

Diagnosis:
_____
_____
_____

Medication - Vaccinations:
_____
_____
_____

Comments:
_____
_____
_____

Vet Visits

Date: _____ Age: _____

Reason for Visit: _____
_____
_____

Tests Done:
_____
_____
_____

Diagnosis:
_____
_____
_____

Medication - Vaccinations:
_____
_____
_____

Comments:
_____
_____
_____

Vet Visits

Date: _____ **Age:** _____

Reason for Visit:
_____
_____

Tests Done:

_____
_____
_____

Diagnosis:

_____
_____
_____

Medication - Vaccinations:

_____
_____
_____

Comments:

_____
_____
_____

Vet Visits

Date: _____ Age: _____

Reason for Visit: _____

_____

_____

Tests Done:

_____

_____

_____

Diagnosis:

_____

_____

_____

Medication - Vaccinations:

_____

_____

_____

Comments:

_____

_____

_____

Vet Visits

Date: _____ Age: _____

Reason for Visit:
_____

_____

Tests Done:
_____

_____

_____

Diagnosis:
_____

_____

_____

Medication - Vaccinations:
_____

_____

_____

Comments:
_____

_____

_____

Vet Visits

Date: _____ Age: _____

Reason for Visit: _____

_____

_____

Tests Done:

_____

_____

_____

Diagnosis:

_____

_____

_____

Medication - Vaccinations:

_____

_____

_____

Comments:

_____

_____

_____

Vet Visits

Date:	Age:

Reason for Visit:

Tests Done:

Diagnosis:

Medication - Vaccinations:

Comments:

Vet Visits

Date: _____ Age: _____

Reason for Visit: _____

_____

_____

Tests Done:

_____

_____

_____

Diagnosis:

_____

_____

_____

Medication - Vaccinations:

_____

_____

_____

Comments:

_____

_____

_____

Vet Visits

Date:	Age:

Reason for Visit:

Tests Done:

_____

_____

_____

Diagnosis:

_____

_____

_____

Medication - Vaccinations:

_____

_____

_____

Comments:

_____

_____

_____

Vet Visits

Date: _____   Age: _____

Reason for Visit: _____

_____

_____

Tests Done:

_____

_____

_____

Diagnosis:

_____

_____

_____

Medication - Vaccinations:

_____

_____

_____

Comments:

_____

_____

_____

Vet Visits

Date: _____ Age: _____

Reason for Visit: _____

_____

_____

Tests Done:

_____

_____

_____

Diagnosis:

_____

_____

_____

Medication - Vaccinations:

_____

_____

_____

Comments:

_____

_____

_____

Vet Visits

Date: _____ Age: _____

Reason for Visit: _____

_____

_____

Tests Done:

_____

_____

_____

Diagnosis:

_____

_____

_____

Medication - Vaccinations:

_____

_____

_____

Comments:

_____

_____

_____

Vet Visits

Date: _____ Age: _____

Reason for Visit: _____

_____

_____

Tests Done:

_____

_____

_____

Diagnosis:

_____

_____

_____

Medication - Vaccinations:

_____

_____

_____

Comments:

_____

_____

_____

Vet Visits

Date: _____ Age: _____

Reason for Visit: _____
_____
_____

Tests Done:
_____
_____
_____

Diagnosis:
_____
_____
_____

Medication - Vaccinations:
_____
_____
_____

Comments:
_____
_____
_____

Vet Visits

Date: _____ Age: _____

Reason for Visit: _____

_____

_____

Tests Done:

_____

_____

_____

Diagnosis:

_____

_____

_____

Medication - Vaccinations:

_____

_____

_____

Comments:

_____

_____

_____

Vet Visits

Date: _____ Age: _____

Reason for Visit: _____
_____
_____

Tests Done:
_____
_____
_____

Diagnosis:
_____
_____
_____

Medication - Vaccinations:
_____
_____
_____

Comments:
_____
_____
_____

Vet Visits

Date: _____   Age: _____

Reason for Visit: _____

_____

_____

Tests Done:

_____

_____

_____

Diagnosis:

_____

_____

_____

Medication - Vaccinations:

_____

_____

_____

Comments:

_____

_____

_____

Vet Visits

Date: _____ Age: _____

Reason for Visit: _____

_____

_____

Tests Done:

_____

_____

_____

Diagnosis:

_____

_____

_____

Medication - Vaccinations:

_____

_____

_____

Comments:

_____

_____

_____

Vet Visits

Date: _____ Age: _____

Reason for Visit: _____
_____
_____

Tests Done:
_____
_____
_____

Diagnosis:
_____
_____
_____

Medication - Vaccinations:
_____
_____
_____

Comments:
_____
_____
_____

Vet Visits

Date: _____ Age: _____

Reason for Visit: _____

_____

_____

Tests Done:

_____

_____

_____

Diagnosis:

_____

_____

_____

Medication - Vaccinations:

_____

_____

_____

Comments:

_____

_____

_____

Vet Visits

Date: _____ Age: _____

Reason for Visit: _____

_____

_____

Tests Done:

_____

_____

_____

Diagnosis:

_____

_____

_____

Medication - Vaccinations:

_____

_____

_____

Comments:

_____

_____

_____

Vet Visits

Date: _____ Age: _____

Reason for Visit: _____

_____

_____

Tests Done:

_____

_____

_____

Diagnosis:

_____

_____

_____

Medication - Vaccinations:

_____

_____

_____

Comments:

_____

_____

_____

Vet Visits

Date: _____ Age: _____

Reason for Visit: _____

_____

_____

Tests Done:

_____

_____

_____

Diagnosis:

_____

_____

_____

Medication - Vaccinations:

_____

_____

_____

Comments:

_____

_____

_____